# ISRAEL

## Michael Gallagher

**W**
**FRANKLIN WATTS**
LONDON • SYDNEY

**Designer** Rita Storey
**Editor** Sarah Ridley
**Art Director** Jonathan Hair
**Editor-in-Chief** John C. Miles
**Picture research** Diana Morris

Franklin Watts
338 Euston Road
London NW1 3BH

Franklin Watts Australia
Hachette Children's Books
Level 17/207 Kent Street
Sydney NSW 2000

A CIP catalogue record for this book
is available from the British Library.

Dewey classification number: 915.694

ISBN-10: 0 7496 6669 2
ISBN-13: 978 0 7496 6669 9

Printed in China

Franklin Watts is a division of Hachette Children's Books.

Picture credits
Roger Antrobus/Corbis: 10. ASAP/Rex Features: 7.
Tim Brakemeier/epa/Corbis: 12. Kevin Frayer/AP/Empics: front cover b, 21.
Gaza Press/Rex Features: 9. Hanan Isachar/Corbis: 19. Edi Israel/Rex
Features: front cover tc. Israelimages/Rex Features: 17.
James Marshall/Corbis: 11. Benjamin Rondel/Corbis: 5.
Ricki Rosen/Saba/Corbis: 25, 26. E Sharir/Israel Sun/Rex Features: 22.
Sipa Press/Rex Features: 1, 6, 13, 20, 23, 24. Ray Tang/Rex Features: 15, 16.
TS/Keystone USA/Rex Features: front cover tl. Yi Tzur/Israel Sun/Rex
Features: 14.

*Every attempt has been made to clear copyright. Should there be any
inadvertent omission please apply to the publisher for rectification.*

**Note to parents and teachers:**
Every effort has been made by the Publishers to ensure that the websites in this
book are suitable for children, that they are of the highest educational value, and that
they contain no inappropriate or offensive material. However, because of the nature
of the Internet, it is impossible to guarantee that the contents of these sites will
not be altered. We strongly advise that Internet access is supervised by a
responsible adult.

# CONTENTS

**THE MODERN STATE OF ISRAEL WAS BORN ON** *15 May 1948, in a region once home to the Jews' ancient forebears, the Israelites. Its central purpose is to provide security for today's Jewish people.*

## ANCIENT HISTORY

Israel is a recent creation, but one linked to thousands of years of history. According to the Bible, it was here, on the eastern shores of the Mediterranean, that the Jewish religion first formed, over 3,000 years ago, in a land promised by God. Jewish ancestors, known as the Israelites, built a mighty kingdom and made Jerusalem its capital. Later, the Israelites split into two separate realms which, over the centuries, were invaded by Assyrians, Babylonians, Romans and others. The inhabitants were persecuted and many fled, scattering the Jewish nation far and wide.

## ZIONIST DREAM

For almost 2,000 years, the Jews were then without a country of their own. Instead, they settled throughout much of the world, keeping a strong cultural and religious identity wherever they went. However, they suffered persecution and hostility, especially in Europe. In the 19th century, one group of Jews decided their people could never be safe until they had a land of their own once again. They called themselves Zionists and they began gathering support for a new Jewish state. After much debate, they decided its location should be the site of the ancient Jewish kingdoms.

● These maps show Israel's position in the world.

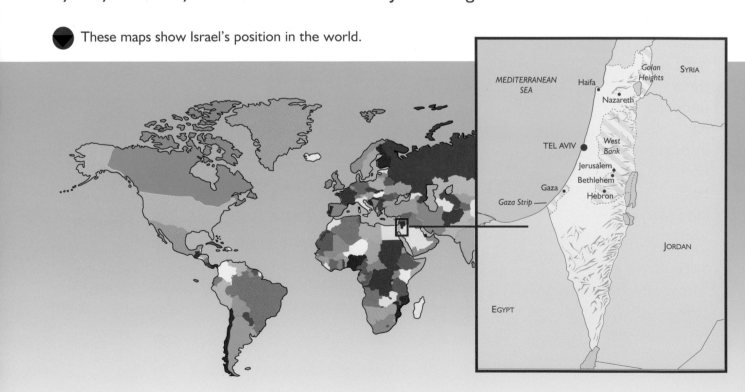

 Israel's landscape is hilly and dry.

## TWO PEOPLES, ONE LAND

The Zionists grew stronger in the 20th century. With the discovery of the Nazi holocaust – Hitler's attempt to kill all the Jews of Europe – their cause seemed unquestionable. However, they faced a major problem as, after 2,000 years, hardly any Jews remained in the land of the ancient Israelites, which was now under British control. The region even had a new name – Palestine. Most important of all, for centuries it had been home to an Arab population. When Zionists began migrating to Palestine to settle the land for Jews, violent clashes broke out with the resident Palestinian Arabs.

## THE BIRTH OF MODERN ISRAEL

The United Nations tried to divide Palestine to keep the peace and, although Jews eventually accepted the idea, the Palestinian Arabs did not want to give up any of their land. Then, in 1948, when the

## KNOW YOUR FACTS

Arabs were not the only ones against the idea of a Jewish state. Some very religious Jews, too, think it was wrong. They believe that Jews should not return to the ancient land of their forefathers until the Messiah – the divine saviour of mankind – arrives on Earth. Even so, many of them choose to live in Israel.

British pulled out of Palestine, the Zionists declared the creation of their new Jewish state anyway, and the modern state of Israel was born. Many thousands of Palestinian Arabs fled their homes, and the Arab world reacted with fury. Immediately, the surrounding Arab countries invaded on behalf of the Palestinians, beginning what the Israelis call their War of Independence. Although Israel won the war, its conflict with the Palestinians burns on to this day, and, ironically, Israel's biggest challenge remains that of security.

Israeli troops in action during the Six Day War in 1967.

**TODAY, ISRAELI JEWS AND PALESTINIAN ARABS** *still die regularly in the ongoing conflict over the Jewish state. With such bitter dispute over the region, even understanding its borders can be hard.*

### A HISTORY OF CONFLICT

The Jewish state of Israel is surrounded by Arab countries: Lebanon and Syria lie to the north, Jordan to the east and Egypt to the south. These neighbours, along with the mainly Muslim Arabs of Palestine, were violently opposed to its creation, which they saw as an occupation of Arab land. During Israel's first three decades, they fought several wars to try and destroy it. However, Israel won every one of them. As a result of one war, in 1967, Israel conquered and occupied even more land, though this has never been internationally recognised as its own.

### SPOILS OF WAR

Today, in addition to its original territory, Israel occupies a number of areas, lying between its original boundaries and the neighbouring Arab states. These areas are known as occupied territories (see map on page 4). In the north, it has annexed from Syria a hilltop area called the Golan Heights, in order to prevent a Syrian invasion. To the south, it controls the airspace and seafront of a thin piece of land next to Egypt, called the Gaza Strip. The biggest occupied territory, however, is the West Bank of the River Jordan. This lies between the river itself and Israel's eastern boundary. The geography of the West Bank is complicated. Some parts are administered by the Palestinian Arabs, who want to establish their own state there, while other parts have been inhabited by Jewish settlers.

## CAPITAL DISPUTE

The West Bank areas settled by Jews include the eastern part of Jerusalem, which the Palestinians hope to make the capital of a future Palestinian state. Before Israel's creation, all of Jerusalem was set aside as international territory. Israel now claims the whole of the city as its own "eternal, undivided capital". However, this does not have international approval and – officially – East Jerusalem belongs to the occupied territories.

## JERUSALEM

Israelis adore Jerusalem. As the centre of the ancient Israelite kingdom, it is said that King David brought the Ark of the Covenant – the symbol of the Jews' special pact with God – here. A temple was built, and later rebuilt, and Jerusalem became the heart of the Jewish faith. Yet the city is also sacred to Christians and Muslims, as the location both of Christ's death, and a miraculous journey to heaven by the Prophet Muhammad. Today Jerusalem remains a mixture of cultures and beliefs. Its most historic part is the walled "old city", which is dominated by the Temple Mount complex – the site of the ancient temples. The Mount's Western – or "Wailing" – Wall (right) is a remnant of the second temple, whose destruction is mourned by the Jews who pray there. It is overlooked by the Muslim mosque called the Dome of the Rock. Throughout its history, Jerusalem has been fought over for both political and religious reasons, and this may well continue. Religious Jews believe that a third temple will be built when the Messiah returns to save mankind. For them, giving up Jerusalem would be like throwing away salvation itself.

**THE NEW CITIZENS OF ISRAEL HAD MANY** *different visions for their new state, but the threat of Arab attack brought them together as one. Today it remains their most pressing concern.*

## AMBITIONS

Although a majority of Jews supported the Zionist dream of a Jewish state, not all of them agreed on exactly what form it should take. For many devout Jews, Israel was a spiritual concept – a return to the ancient land promised by God. But some founders were not interested in religion at all. They were more nationalistic and wanted to create a new image of the Jews as a tough people of action. Others hoped to build a socialist nation, in which the working classes would live in equality with the rich. Given that, by 1948, Jews from some 70 countries had come to a small and – at that time – poor country, it is hardly surprising that Israel inherited such widely differing ideals.

## PALESTINIAN VIOLENCE

What united the different groups more than anything else was the threat from Arabs hostile to the Jewish state. Since its creation in 1948, Israel has been in a constant military struggle, sometimes fighting for its very survival. At first, the main danger was from surrounding Arab countries, which invaded to support the displaced Palestinians. Now, Israel has made peace with most of its neighbours, but the Palestinians themselves have

## KNOW YOUR FACTS

The term "Palestinian" did not exist as we know it until the creation of Israel. Previously, Arabs living in Palestine considered themselves part of the wider Arab nation. The dawn of the Jewish state, though, singled them out as perceived victims, which led them to feel like a separate people. Palestinian nationalism is further strengthened by the shared hope of one day having their own country.

become the main enemy. Over the years, Israelis have become used to attacks against soldiers and civilians alike, including suicide bombings against soft targets, such as shopping centres, bus stations and restaurants. Although Israel has always mounted a tough military response, it has never been able to put a complete stop to the violence. Also, many Palestinians complain bitterly of injustice at the hands of Israeli troops, and foreign governments have sometimes criticised Israel for being heavy-handed.

## SWORN ENEMIES

Today, Israel's Palestinian opponents have a degree of self-rule, including the ability to elect leaders to represent them. In 2006, their elections were won by the Islamic resistance movement, Hamas, which was created to destroy Israel by force and to replace it with a Muslim

 Four million Palestinians are now classed as refugees. Many, such as these people, live in semi-permanent refugee settlements and rely on aid to survive.

Palestinian state. Hamas has been responsible for many of the suicide bombs in Israel, and most Israelis see it as a terrorist group. The hope is still that, one day, the Palestinians will have their own state, based in the West Bank and Gaza, and live side by side with Israel in peace. But in the meantime, it seems the conflict between Arabs and Jews will continue to leave its mark on Israel.

## GROUNDS FOR DEBATE

In 1950, Israel's "Law of Return" granted any Jew from any country the right to migrate to Israel and thus "return" to the holy land. As a result, today's Israelis are descendants of settlers from over 100 different countries. Palestinian refugees, who fled their homes in the fighting when Israel was created, also want to return. But if Israel allowed this, it would no longer be a majority Jewish state. So, who should have the right of return?

# GEOGRAPHY: SMALL AND BEAUTIFUL

**ISRAEL'S COUNTRYSIDE IS MODEST IN SIZE,** *but impressive all the same. Yet, until there is peace with the Palestinians, it is likely to be scarred.*

## DOT ON THE LANDSCAPE

Visitors to Israel are often surprised by how close everything is, for it is a tiny country – about the size of Wales in the UK, or the state of New Jersey, USA. It contains four distinct geographical areas. There is a thin, fertile plain in the west, running along Israel's long Mediterranean coast. Behind this, highlands rise, which are especially mountainous in the northern Galilee region. A rift valley runs through the east, where the famous River Jordan flows into the Dead Sea. Finally,

● The Dead Sea is actually an inland lake but contains water with such a high salt content that people can float in it without any effort.

the hot, dry Negev Desert lies to the south. Desert accounts for more than half of Israel's land area.

Israel's climate is Mediterranean, with warm dry summers and cooler, wet winters, though more northerly and higher locations can be quite cold. In winter, it is possible to ski in the mountains of Galilee, or sunbathe in Eilat!

## MAKING THE MOST OF IT

Israel has few natural resources like oil or coal, but its people have worked very hard to improve their land and make it a source of wealth. Today, the country is largely self-sufficient in food, and its economy has grown too; once relatively poor and undeveloped, it now enjoys a standard of living similar to western Europe. The vibrant city of Tel Aviv, with

 Over half of Israel's area is taken up by desert.

its skyscrapers and pleasure beaches, is just one example of modern living amid all the history of this ancient region.

## NEW CONSTRUCTION

There is, however, a darker side to Israel's geography. In the far north, the Golan Heights remain annexed to prevent invasion from Syria. Crossing points to other neighbouring countries are heavily fortified. And, most notoriously, what the government calls its new security fence has recently sprouted up inside the West Bank. This is a barrier, dividing Palestinians from those areas of the occupied territory most heavily settled by Jews. In parts, it is as wide as a motorway, and concrete walls up to eight metres high run along some of its length. The barrier is meant to protect Israel and some of its West Bank settlements from

## KNOW YOUR FACTS

Israel has minimal natural resources, so its economy is focused on making things rather than extracting them from the Earth. Following years of difficulty, the country began enjoying an economic boom in 2004. One of its best assets is its labour force. Thanks to mass immigration – especially from the former Soviet Union – workers are plentiful and highly skilled. Israel is also the biggest recipient in the world of US foreign aid. However, it spends around a quarter of its income on defence.

Palestinian attacks. But critics say it often prevents Palestinians accessing their own property. There is concern, too, that Israel may claim it as its permanent international border, annexing West Bank land in the process.

**THE EVIL OF THE HOLOCAUST SERVES AS A LESSON** *for all mankind. It has also taught the Jews of Israel never to be weak in the face of their enemies.*

## RESOLUTE NATION

The Israelis are a tough people – too tough, according to their critics. Some native-born citizens compare themselves to sabra – the local cactus fruit which, while sweet on the inside, is thick-skinned and thorny. Part of the reason for this resilience is the seemingly endless Palestinian conflict. But to fully understand the Israeli mindset, we must also consider the holocaust of the Second World War, just before Israel was created. At least six million Jews were systematically murdered by Nazi Germany, in an attempt to wipe out their entire population in Europe. The *shoah*, as Israelis call it, proved the need for the Jewish state, and for it to be invincible.

 An Auschwitz death camp survivor relives the horrors of the shoah at a ceremony to commemorate the liberation of the camp.

## GROUNDS FOR DEBATE

The six million victims are not alive to benefit from remembrance, and even many Jews who survived the Nazis have since died of old age. So why is it so important for Israel – and the wider world – to commemorate the holocaust? What do you think about people who argue that we should move on and forget?

## TURNING POINT

For years, Israelis could hardly bring themselves to talk about the holocaust – it was so traumatic. What has helped the nation come to terms with the tragedy was the capture of former Nazi officer, Adolf Eichmann, in 1960. As one of the chief co-ordinators of the holocaust, he had fled to Argentina to hide after the war. Israeli secret agents snatched him from a street and smuggled him back to Israel, where he was put on trial. To see one of their former tormentors brought to justice by a Jewish court in a Jewish state was a hugely significant moment for most Israelis. In 1962, Eichmann was hanged for his crimes.

## NEVER FORGOTTEN

Today, the holocaust remains a defining feature of Israeli society. There are still Israelis who can recall friends and relatives who perished at the hands of the Nazis. Many of them narrowly escaped death themselves. In Israeli newspapers, barely a day goes by without some mention of the holocaust. Visiting foreign dignitaries are always taken to Jerusalem's Yad Vashem memorial, where an eternal flame burns in memory of the victims. Some people believe Israel's preoccupation with the holocaust is exploited. They say some politicians compare Palestinian enemies to the Nazis in order to justify harsh action

against them; but such views appear to be a minority. Opinion polls have suggested that most Israelis – even those with no personal connection to the genocide – consider themselves to be holocaust survivors.

Israelis will always remember the holocaust's six million Jewish victims. This eternal flame burns at Yad Vashem, the holocaust memorial in Jerusalem.

**AT UNDER SEVEN MILLION, ISRAEL'S POPULATION IS SMALL,** *yet it is one of the most varied of any country. Though it includes many immigrants, all Israelis have in common a close bond with their country's land and its history.*

## ARABS AND JEWS

Today, Israeli society is made up of all the different groups who helped create the state, plus many more that did not. Half the population was born overseas and migrated to Israel in more recent years. Around a fifth of citizens are not even Jewish, mostly the descendants of the 100,000 mainly Muslim Arabs who did not leave the area after 1948.

## HEBREW

Hebrew was the language of the ancient Israelites, but for centuries it was largely unspoken, until a Lithuanian scholar, Eliezer Ben-Yehuda, revived it after 1885. He compiled a dictionary, including thousands of new words from Hebrew roots to describe the modern world. In 1948 Modern Hebrew was adopted as the official language of Israel, and since then it has evolved further, influenced by immigrants' national languages and Yiddish, the traditional Ashkenazi tongue.

The entire Jewish community of Ethiopia, along with its unusual religious customs, has now been absorbed into Israel.

Israel's relaxed Mediterranean culture is centred on the city of Tel Aviv.

Almost four million Arabs live, without Israeli citizenship but under Israeli control, in the occupied territories. Christian and other minorities also exist, including some foreign guest workers.

## ASHKENAZIM AND SEPHARDIM

Among Jewish citizens, there is much diversity too. Those of eastern and central European descent, known as the Ashkenazim, live alongside the culturally distinct Sephardim, whose ancestors came from Iberia, North Africa and the Middle East. The Sephardim often maintain customs influenced by Arab culture, and usually follow traditional Jewish practices. Ashkenazi Jews tend to be much less middle ground, as they are often either extremely religious or not very religious at all. Other Jewish groups

are different again – the customs of black Ethiopian "Falasha" Jews are so unusual that they even had trouble proving their Jewishness in order to come to Israel.

## SECULAR AND RELIGIOUS

About half the population does not worship regularly. Many Israeli youngsters travel overseas, to countries like the United States, and bring home western influences. Popular culture thrives in places like Tel Aviv, where nightclubs and pavement cafés are often more apparent than places of worship. Some Israelis view such merriment with alarm. They believe it could undermine the national unity that has kept Israel strong. How to enable all citizens to enjoy their lives without letting down their guard is a big challenge facing Israeli society.

*ISRAEL'S DECLARATION OF INDEPENDENCE guarantees freedom of worship for all faiths. Nevertheless, Judaism is effectively an official religion in Israel.*

### CHOSEN PEOPLE

Judaism is much older than Christianity and Islam, both of which it heavily influenced, as it traces its teachings back some 3,500 years, to the time before the ancient kingdom of the Israelites.

According to Jewish teaching, there is one God who created the universe. In return for obeying His laws, given to the prophet Moses, the Jews have a special relationship with Him. Jews believe that God led their ancestors through the wilderness to the promised land of Israel, and that He will favour them again when the day of judgement comes.

### ANCIENT AND MODERN

Although only a minority of Israelis belong to the highly traditional, so-called Orthodox Jewish groups, these have a very influential role in the nation's religious life. They ensure that the Sabbath is widely observed, with no public transport and most businesses closed. Their religious institutions receive generous subsidies from the government, and exercise a high degree of control over personal and family affairs. For instance, in Israel, all marriages are religious, rather than civil. In addition, a Jewish woman may not remarry, even if her husband disappears, unless a religious court declares a divorce. There are various sub-groups within the Orthodox tradition, but all are characterised by a strict interpretation of Jewish law, including dress code, diet and religious ritual.

Other worshipping communities within Judaism, such as the Liberal, Reform and Conservative movements, consider

 A boy helps carry a Torah scroll as part of his Bar Mitzvah, or coming of age ceremony.

This modern Sephardic synagogue is in Tel Aviv.

themselves more progressive, and try to interpret the ancient scriptures in the light of the modern world. Reform Judaism for example, allows females to play a much greater role in worship.

## IN COMMUNION WITH GOD

Despite their differences, all practising Jews carry out the same basic acts of devotion. They pray three times a day, follow the religious calendar of feasts, fasts and worship, and eat only "kosher" (properly prepared) food. The Sabbath, (or Shabbat), between the Friday and Saturday sunsets, is very special. It symbolises the seventh day upon which God rested, after creating the world, and

A Jew is considered to be anyone born of a Jewish mother, provided they have not adopted any other faith. Playing a full part in the community takes more time though. Boys start their adult religious life aged 13-and-a-day, by undergoing the Bar Mitzvah coming-of-age ritual. Non-Orthodox girls can have a Bat Mitzvah aged 12-and-a-day. Non-Jews, or Gentiles, may convert to Judaism, though this is not an easy process.

Jews, too, put down their work. Shabbat in Israel is a very quiet time as Jews commit themselves to their families, contemplation and prayer.

# 8 THE KIBBUTZ

**ISRAEL'S COMMUNAL FARMS, THE KIBBUTZIM,** *sum up the country's pioneering spirit and the classless ideals of some of its people.*

## TAMING THE LAND

The kibbutz (plural: kibbutzim) is unique to Israel, although the idea first emerged in the 1900s, before Israel was created. Kibbutzim are small communities, each one jointly owned by all its members. Most began life as farms, with the aim of forging deep links between Zionist Jews and the land of their ancestors. The kibbutzim are credited with much of the back-breaking effort to develop Israel's agricultural land, some of which had been badly neglected before 1948. They drained swamps and watered arid soils and, as a popular saying puts it, "made the desert bloom".

## SHARE AND CARE

Today there are still around 300 kibbutzim, typically with between 50 and 1,000 members. They are all based on the principle of equality for, on a kibbutz, everything is shared: work, property, income, mealtimes, decision-making – and more. The community ideology is so strong that even the family takes second place. Members participate in educating children born on the kibbutz, and, traditionally, they even shared the parenting itself, with youngsters cared for in a "baby house" rather than living with their birth-parents.

## ADAPT OR DIE

However, kibbutzim are having to change with the times. Today the conventional family is making a comeback and the baby house is gone. Also, in our consumer age, fewer people are willing to live without personal possessions and many kibbutz members now get a financial allowance to spend outside their community. Indeed, some kibbutzim have effectively become private companies.

Many have moved into industrial rather than agricultural production, making anything from processed foods to electrical goods. Others, once in the countryside but now close to expanded urban areas, have moved into providing

## KNOW YOUR FACTS

The moshav (plural: moshavim) is another type of rural co-operative, but one with more independence for its members. Unlike the traditional kibbutz, it is made up of individual families who live separately. They may work shared land or their own farms, but in either case they unite to sell their produce and buy essentials. Moshavim were often dependent on Palestinian labour, but in response to security concerns, many have now turned to migrant workers from as far away as Thailand.

Workers on a kibbutz tend fruit trees.

## HELPING OUT

Young adults from all over the world can share the kibbutz experience, since external volunteers contribute to the labour force of most kibbutzim. Those taking part typically work at least six hours a day, six days a week, and receive only a small allowance for their efforts. Some say they will never repeat the experience but many others are deeply moved by the spirit of comradeship they encounter.

services like laundering clothes. Some people believe that the kibbutzim have abandoned their old principles. Yet a large number of children born on kibbutzim still choose to continue living there as adults, ensuring the ideals of communal living survive into a fourth generation of Israelis.

Many settlements, like this one, contain well-established neighbourhoods.

**OVER THE LAST FOUR DECADES, SOME JEWS** *have begun living outside official Israeli territory, in occupied territories like the West Bank. The rest of Israel has mixed opinions about them.*

Take a look around the occupied territories, and you will often see bright, modern housing developments, glistening in the sunshine. These are Jewish settlements, illegal under international law, but now home to more than 400,000 Jews in total (including East Jerusalem).

## FOR GOD OR THE GOOD LIFE
Settlers have a variety of reasons for living on occupied land. Some were coaxed there by the government to create new towns that would help defend Israel against invasion. Some simply want affordable housing, and are attracted by a lower cost of living and state incentives such as cheap loans and childcare. Others, though, are extremely religious. They refer to the West Bank by its biblical names of Judea and Samaria, and believe it belongs to them by divine right, as part of the ancient Jewish holy land. Settlers like these consider themselves to be champions of Judaism, guiding an Israel which they see as ungodly.

## UNDER FIRE

Whatever their motives, many settlers find themselves in danger in their new homes. The Palestinians are enraged by their presence. They believe it proves Israel will never move out of the occupied territories. As a result, settlers have become frequent targets for Palestinian gunmen who seek to drive them out. So, to be a settler often means living behind barbed wire, travelling on armoured buses and keeping a gun at the ready, night and day. Many settlements have to have their own roads, which Palestinians are not allowed to use. Permanently stationed Israeli soldiers add to the state of siege.

## NO WAY BACK

Not all Israelis approve of this. Some resent the money that needs to be spent defending the settlers. Others think settlers are fanatics. Still more believe settlements stand in the way of peace. Increased Palestinian violence has persuaded some non-religious settlers to consider moving out. However, among the religious ones, there certainly seems little appetite for change. In 2005, the government ordered all 8,000 Jewish settlers to leave the Gaza Strip, as part of a plan to concentrate settlement in the West Bank. Many complained loudly, and a determined minority had to be carried away from their homes by soldiers.

● A pro-settlements protester is forcibly moved by police at a demonstration.

**GIVEN THE CONSTANT THREAT OF ATTACK SINCE ISRAEL'S BIRTH**, *the army is one of the country's most important institutions. In addition to its military role, it also plays a big part in society itself.*

### A DUTY FOR ALL

Few armies are closer to the people they serve than Israel's. The Israeli Defence Force, or IDF, is considered unique, as it is made up largely of the citizens themselves. Doing national service is a major rite of passage for most young people – boys and girls alike. Typically, conscripts enlist for two or three years of basic training. Then, they join the reserve list for up to 30 years, to be called up if the need arises. Even as reservists, they do more than a month of active service every year.

### BACKBONE OF THE NATION

Because of its crucial role and because so many people contribute to it, the IDF is seen as a great institution. Many people believe it has helped overcome a feeling of vulnerability that Jews once had, helping to build national pride and morale. It also acts as a unifier for Israeli society, which is especially important in a country made up of so many immigrants from different backgrounds. Military service includes education in subjects like Jewish studies, modern Hebrew and Israeli history, enabling conscripts to develop a common culture.

The IDF trains for combat in all conditions, including mountain snow.

Two Israeli soldiers on manoeuvres help a female colleague with her heavy pack.

## CHANGING TIMES

Of course, the army is not without its problems. In fact, the very solidarity it provides for most people can serve to distance others. For a start, Arab citizens of Israel are not required to serve in the same way as Jews, although they may volunteer if they wish. And some Orthodox Jews claim exemption from military service on religious grounds, stirring resentment among the wider population. Even more challenging is that young people's attitudes towards army life seem to be changing. Although Israel is still constantly skirmishing with Palestinian gunmen, it is no longer fighting for its very survival, as it was some years ago. As a result, IDF conscripts

## KNOW YOUR FACTS

The IDF grew out of a number of underground Jewish militias formed before Israel's creation, when Palestine was under the control of the British. Its main forerunner was Haganah – a force set up to repel Arab attacks and mount retaliatory campaigns. After Haganah became the IDF, other paramilitaries were integrated into the new army, including members of the Lehi and Irgun groups, which had previously targeted British interests.

sometimes feel freer to criticise the old way of doing things. There are people who think that, in today's world, Israel should have a professional military, like other countries. Yet such a force would doubtless be much smaller than the traditional citizen reserve army. Until Israel feels completely safe from violence, it is not likely to opt for that.

# GOVERNMENT AND FOREIGN RELATIONS

**ISRAEL PRIDES ITSELF ON BEING** *the Middle East's most stable and democratic country. Yet, within the international community, the Jewish state has its critics.*

### NEW ARRIVAL

For almost 60 years, Israeli governments were invariably led by one of two main political parties. First, the Labour party was in charge, but from 1977 its more conservative rival, Likud, tended to be more powerful. Then, in 2005, Israeli politics was turned on its head when prime minister Ariel Sharon declared that he was forming an entirely new political party called Kadima. Kadima is positioned to occupy the centre ground between Labour and Likud, and politicians from both the established main parties have joined. In the general election of March 2006 – the first one it ever contested – Kadima won the most votes, defeating the once mighty Likud party.

## KADIMA

Kadima's creation in November 2005 was a shock - its founder was leading the Likud party at the time! Ariel Sharon's decision was sparked by a new attempt to end the Palestinian conflict: Kadima seeks a negotiated settlement, but says it will impose one if this does not succeed. Ironically, whatever happens, Mr Sharon will not be in charge: soon after starting the new party his political career was cut short by a stroke.

A former mayor of Jerusalem, Ehud Olmert became leader of the new Kadima party after Ariel Sharon's illness.

## UNITED STATES

Israel's international politics has also changed over the years. Because of external threats, Israel has always looked overseas for support. Once, France was its preferred partner, supplying arms and the technical know-how for an Israeli nuclear weapons programme. Today, Israel's most important ally is, by far, the United States. Ever since the 1973 Arab-Israeli War, when American weapons saved Israel from defeat, the two countries have maintained extremely close ties. For Israel, this has meant an estimated $1.6 trillion US in loans and grants – no other country receives so much US foreign aid.

## THE ARAB WORLD

Beyond the US, some countries are more ready to criticise Israel. In particular, Arab and Muslim states are often wary of having close relations. Most of them are no longer publicly committed to destroying the Jewish state as they once were. Indeed Israel now enjoys full diplomatic relations with its Arab neighbours, Jordan and Egypt. But the Arab world is keenly aware that much of its public remains angry. A few – like Syria and Iran – are suspected of plotting against Israel to this day. Iran in particular is accused of sponsoring groups like Hezbollah, which attacks Israeli soldiers and civilians.

## KNOW YOUR FACTS

Choosing an Israeli government looks simple – in theory. In proportion to the votes it receives, each political party wins seats in the 120-member parliament, called the Knesset. Anyone with more than two per cent of the nation's votes can get a seat, so the Knesset tends to be made up of many different parties. This means every government is a coalition, or alliance, of several different parties, and Israeli politicians have to haggle and bargain constantly.

Like the country itself, politics in Israel can be passionate and fiery.

# THE FUTURE

**AS A VERY YOUNG NATION, IT IS LIKELY** *that Israel will continue to develop rapidly, just as it has done since 1948. Meanwhile, its politicians believe they can end the conflict over its country's borders once and for all.*

## LAST OF THE NEW ARRIVALS

Israel's population will now probably remain stable. There are not likely to be any more big migrations to absorb, as most of the world's Jews not already in Israel live in the United States, where they appear to be quite settled. Instead,

Large migrations to Israel, like the one these Russian Jews joined in the 1990s, are unlikely in the future.

the existing people, descended from over 100 different countries, will have to continue growing together, merging all their differences into a common Israeli nationhood. The big question is how Jewish this nation will be.

## REDRAWING THE BORDERS

Without big Jewish influxes from overseas, there is concern within Israel that its spirit and energy may be lost, especially if people forget the early national struggle to establish the state. Worse, according to some, is that Jews in Israel and the occupied territories may one day be outnumbered by Palestinians. For this

reason, politicians of the Kadima party want to withdraw from those parts of the occupied West Bank where most Arabs live, while keeping forever the areas heavily settled by Jews. Kadima aims to carry out this "separation plan" and fix permanent borders for Israel by 2010.

### INEVITABLE ANGER

This vision will certainly not be easy to realise. Palestinians and many in the international community say Israel should return all the occupied territories, not just some of them. Already, there is protest that some West Bank areas have been enclosed by the new security barrier, as if they were part of Israel.

Even more difficult will be dealing with the rage of Jewish settlers who will have to leave their homes elsewhere in the West Bank. As the years go by, more and more residents are actually born in settlements, and they will have to give up the only life they have ever known. In 2006, the Kadima leader, Ehud Olmert, said he would try to overcome all the objections by negotiation. But, he added, if this fails, Kadima will go ahead anyway.

Whether or not the separation plan succeeds will depend on many things, not least the ups and downs of Israeli politics. But given both the difficulties and the determination of Israel and its people, it seems probable that this country's short-term future, like its past, will be one of controversy.

## GROUNDS FOR DEBATE

In a famous declaration of 1967 called Resolution 242, the United Nations called upon Israel to withdraw from all the occupied territories. Palestinians say that by not doing so, Israel is ignoring the international community. The Israelis argue that Resolution 242 demands withdrawal only as part of an overall settlement with the Palestinians. They say it also calls for their enemies to leave them in peace. What do you think?

## WATER

A growing challenge to Israel is the lack of water in the country. It has one of the lowest supplies per head in the world. There has been talk of importing water from Turkey, hundreds of kilometres to the north, but this would be very expensive. Other possibilities include taking more from the River Jordan. Meanwhile, Israel gets up to a third of its water from the occupied Golan Heights. If the scarcity continues, some commentators say water could replace land as the main reason for conflict in the region.

**1948:** **14th May** David Ben-Gurion proclaims an independent state of Israel, to come into force the next day as the last British troops pull out of Palestine.

**1948: 15th May** Arab armies enter Palestine and Israel. Israel's "War of Independence" lasts until January 1949.

**1950:** The Knesset adopts the Law of Return, allowing any Jew the right to live in Israel.

**1956:** The start of the Israeli invasion of Egypt, with British and French help.

**1967:** The "Six Day War" between Israel and its Arab neighbours. Israel occupies the West Bank, East Jerusalem, Gaza Strip, Golan Heights and Sinai peninsula (later returned).

**1968:** Rabbi Moshe Levinger and his supporters celebrate Passover in the West Bank town of Hebron, later refusing to leave, and paving the way for a host of religious settlements.

**1972:** Eleven killed in an attack on Israeli athletes at the Munich Olympic Games.

**1973:** "Yom Kippur War" between Israel and the Arabs which lasts until 11th November.

**1978:** Israel and Egypt finally agree to live in peace.

**1980:** Israel declares all of Jerusalem to be its undivided and eternal capital.

**1982:** "Operation Peace for Galilee" – Israel launches a full-scale invasion of Lebanon.

**1987:** The start of the first "intifada" Palestinian uprising in the occupied territories.

**1989:** The Islamic resistance group, Hamas, is outlawed.

**1990:** Jews begin leaving the Soviet Union to live in Israel. Israel vows to find homes for all who migrate.

**1993:** Hopes for peace between Israel and the Palestinians reach an all-time high as both sides sign the Oslo Peace Accord at the White House in Washington, USA.

**1994:** Jordan makes peace with Israel.

**1995:** The pro-peace Israeli prime minister, Yitzhak Rabin, is murdered by a Jewish extremist. The Oslo Peace Accord begins to break down.

**2000:** The Israeli premier, Ehud Barak, completes the full withdrawal from Lebanon.

**2000:** The future prime minister, Ariel Sharon, tours the Temple Mount/haram al Sharif in Jerusalem. The start of the second "intifada" Palestinian uprising.

**2002:** Pro-Palestinian attacks kill over a hundred Israelis.

**2003:** The publication of the "Road Map" for peace, by the US, UN, European Union and Russia.

**2004:** Israel assassinates the Hamas spiritual leader, Sheikh Ahmed Yassin.

**2005:** Likud prime minister, Ariel Sharon, leaves to set up the Kadima party.

**2006:** Hamas wins the Palestinian elections.

# BASIC FACTS

**POPULATION:** 6,700,000 (UN 2005) – of whom, Jews 5,200,000/non-Jews 1,500,000.

**LANGUAGES:** Hebrew and Arabic. English widely spoken.

**MAJOR RELIGIONS:** Judaism and Islam. Also Christian, Druze and other minorities.

**SEAT OF GOVERNMENT:** Jerusalem (disputed).

**LAND AREA:** 22,072 square kilometres (including Jerusalem).

**GNI (GROSS NATIONAL INCOME):** US$17,380 per head (World Bank, 2005).

**CURRENCY:** New Israeli Shekel (NIS) 1 NIS=100 new agorot

**MAJOR INDUSTRIES**: Computer software, military equipment, chemicals, agriculture and tourism.

**LIFE EXPECTANCY**: 76.7 (males); 80.9 (females).

**Abraham** A biblical character. Jews believe his son Isaac is the ancestor of their nation. Muslims say his other son, Ishmail, is the father of the Arab nation.

**Annex** To take possession and absorb an area of land into a state, especially without the legal right to do so.

**Arabs** A mainly Muslim people who share the Arabic language. Arabs originated in the Arabian Peninsula but migrated throughout the Middle East and North Africa following the birth of Islam in the 7th century.

**Citizen** A person entitled to be a full member of a state.

**Conscript** A person who must do compulsory military service.

**Conservative Judaism** A form of Judaism in which some changes to the traditional way of doing things are allowed.

**Genocide** The deliberate killing of an entire race or nation.

**Holocaust** The attempt by Nazi Germany to murder all of Europe's Jews. Some six million of them died as a result, including one-and-a-half million children. The holocaust also targeted gypsies, the disabled and others.

**Kosher** Fulfilling the requirements of Jewish law. Kosher food, for example, must conform to a number of rules including proper slaughter, with all blood drained out, and the separate preparation and storage of meat and dairy produce.

**Messiah** The promised saviour of mankind, whom devout Jews believe will rebuild the Temple in Jerusalem and deliver them from their enemies.

**Nation** A people sharing common descent, history and customs. Not to be confused with a state (see below).

**Observant Jews** Those who follow the laws and customs of Judaism.

**Occupied territories** The Gaza Strip, Golan Heights, West Bank and East Jerusalem, which Israel conquered in 1967. Israel has now moved its settlers out of Gaza, though it still holds a lot of control over the area.

**Orthodox Jew** A person observing very traditional, unaltered Jewish laws and customs.

**Palestine** The name once given to the region in which Israel now stands. Palestinians say Israel occupies 78 per cent of Palestine, with the occupied territories making up the other 22 per cent. However, there was never any strict definition of Palestine's exact land area.

**Palestinian** A member of Palestine's former Arab population, or one of their descendents.

**Reform Judaism**  A type of Judaism which accepts certain changes to Jewish ritual based upon modern developments in science and philosophy.

**Rift valley**  A steep valley formed by a break in the Earth's crust.

**Secular**  Non-religious.

**State**  The political apparatus of government, defence and police associated with a country.

**Suicide bomb**  A bomb attack delivered to the target by a person who agrees to die in the process. Suicide bombs can therefore achieve a much greater degree of accuracy and surprise.

**Zionism**  The worldwide movement to establish the modern state of Israel. Zionism takes its name from Zion, the hill upon which Jerusalem's temples once stood.

# WEBSITES

**www.goisrael.com**
The website of Israel's Ministry of Tourism.

**www.haaretzdaily.com**
The website of the English language Israeli newspaper, *Haaretz*, with news and features.

**www.mfa.gov.il/mfa**
The official website of the Israeli Foreign Ministry.

**www.bbc.co.uk/news**
The website containing BBC news, with up to the minute coverage of Israel, and links and searches to in-depth articles.

**www.israelradio.org/english.html**
The website of Israel Radio International, with downloads of English language news from the Israel Broadcasting Authority.

**www.knesset.gov.il/main/eng/home.asp**
The English language homepage of the Knesset, Israel's parliament.

**www.yadvashem.org**
The website of Jerusalem's Yad Vashem holocaust memorial.